WHY LOVE HURTS
AND WHY SELF-LOVE IS THE KEY

CONTENTS

INTRO

Why love hurts ... and why self-love is the key is a book that has been inspired by both my personal and my professional journeys. Love is often the cause, but also the cure, of our pain. We might not know it but, beneath the headline hurts that may bring us into therapy at some point in our lifetime, it is likely that an absence of safe, consistent love in our formative years is the root cause. It is my ambition as a therapist to reveal how this absence - in a multiplicity of ways – have made us the people that we are today; how our present distress is fueled by the unresolved hurts of earlier years; how our unhealed pain has shaped our feelings of self-worth. Self-worth is defined as 'the sense of one's own value or worth as a person', so if love was in short supply when we were younger, or if we were treated unkindly or even brutally, it is only natural that our self-worth will be compromised. My goal is to bring to light these past experiences, so that together we can inspect them at a deeper level and, in doing so, free ourselves from the mind-shackles that hold us back. I hope that this book will move you to go beyond reading, to be proactive in bringing self-love practices into your precious life.

I begin by looking, in Chapter 2, at the meaning of self-love, and why it is so crucial. Self-love is a widely used term that most people really don't get. We are often confused about how it looks and feels in reality. In essence, it is about the way that we treat ourselves, which in turn informs how we allow others to treat us. In this context, I explore the importance, for me, of offering myself unconditional love, respect, appreciation and acceptance – all the qualities that I used to give away in abundance to selfish people and never once considered offering to myself (which is often the core reason why romantic love can hurt so much). My psychotherapeutic training put an end to selfless giving and, over four long years, I learned a number of invaluable life lessons including the value of self-compassion and personal boundaries. It is my hope that this book will go some way to assisting you in doing the same. **Self-love really is the key.**

In Chapter 3, Get woke: self-awareness is no joke, I make it clear that self-awareness is fundamental to our efforts to love others and ourselves. In Chapter 4, Wants and needs: know the difference, I use the story of Maggie to show that what we want is not always what we need. Chapter 5, Breaking cycles, encourages a recognition that repeating unhelpful patterns keeps us playing mediocre and robs us of a fulfilling life; we come to see that our relationships are a window through which we can observe our personal progress. Chapter 6, The road to self-love, emphasises that self-love is a journey, and one on which we can only learn to love ourselves through patience, continued practice and hard-won victories. Chapters 7, 8 and 9 focus on the biggest threats to achieving our full potential - our internal and environmental worlds. If left unchecked, these will act as blocks to our progress in a multiplicity of ways, so we need to expect them, and strategise against them. Believe it or not, they are there to test us, and can firm up our determination to succeed.

In Chapters 10, 11 and 12, Self-love audit, I get rather practical and encourage you to audit the three most important areas of your life: your phone, your relationships, and your career. Paying attention to these three aspects will give you important insights and will highlight where (and if) you are 'selling yourself short'. In the chapter after that, Working on the self, I point to the obstacles that you may encounter from unexpected quarters, as you start to say yes to yourself. The final four chapters look at the actual process of personal change, and at the choices and challenges that it presents. I show how self-awareness can be joyous as well as frustrating, and how being 'woke' facilitates meaningful progress. In my closing comments, I pay homage to the people who have entrusted me with their pain and anguish. I suggest that unworthiness is often at the root of our struggles, and that a sense of self-worth is the only way forward. We must believe that we are worthy of better.

◆ ◆ ◆

My personal journey is rather an interesting one, and over the years I have come to realise that people are curious about my story. So here goes. How did I get from being an unskilled checkout cashier, lacking in confidence and with a predictably bleak future, to becoming a successful psychotherapist, business owner, YouTuber and inspirational speaker - in just a little over a decade? If I told you that loving someone hurt me profoundly, and that **self-love** was a fundamental factor in my personal growth and success, would you believe me? Would it seem too far-fetched? Or too good to be true? Well, self-love radically changed my life and it could do the same for you, too.

I am a hardworking, caring, passionate psychotherapist and known for being a change agent for my clients, leaving them inspired, motivated and empowered to transform their lives. I have an ability to wake people up, and clients seek me out for my straight-talking, no-nonsense therapy and coaching services. With a roster of national and international clients, I am fast becoming a sought-after therapist. My straight-to-the-point, short, sharp, thought-provoking videos are known for delivering hard-hitting truths that shake people up. I inspire people to see how their small and seemingly insignificant choices result in their screwing themselves over and selling themselves short. My own life, though, wasn't always as it is now. In 2001, I was at the checkout, scanning candles and blue bags at Ikea. 11 years later, by 2012, I had a BSc in Psychology from Brunel University, completed an MSc in person centered psychotherapy from the world-leading Metanoia Institute in London, and was working full time at Wormwood Scrubs prison as a group facilitator – and all of this was achieved whilst bringing up two wonderful children as a single mother. In 2012 I also founded my London-based psychotherapy, counselling and coaching practice, Key for Change.

I have a solid understanding of the internal and external conditions that both promote and hinder human potential. The impact of external conditions can be extensive. We are constantly inspired, controlled, manipulated and influenced by our environments: political, cultural and technological ones, and those that are based on class, race and social status, to name just a few. The other conditions will be internal factors, those influences that inform and inspire our psychological world view - our beliefs, thoughts, feelings and emotions. Naturally, as a therapist, I am always intrigued by the psychological world of my clients. I am forever curious about how we respond and react to the challenges and demands of the external world. I want to understand how my clients feel about themselves. I want to discover the sources of their sense of self-worth, and their regard (or lack of it) for themselves. For me, there is an intimate relationship between self-worth and self-love, and in my therapeutic work I pay close attention to whether and how self-love manifests itself in a person's life.

I believe that self-love is one of the key qualities that enables us to live fulfilled, wholesome lives. In my view, it is fundamental for us to be willing to invest in ourselves, so that we can unlock the great potential held within each and every one of us. We cannot contract out this work and yes, we will need trusted confidants along the journey, however it's a highly personal walk and only we can save ourselves. Back in 2008, when I used to deliver the Thinking Skills Programme to high-risk offenders, I would often say to the men: 'the most valuable thing you own is in-between your earlobes'. **The truth is, you are your greatest asset, and you never lose when you invest in you**. Watch any of my You-Tube videos. Underlying every video is a theme of self-love and self-responsibility, and every outro says: 'Take care of you, because if you don't – who will?' We must learn to be our own best friend. If not, we risk becoming our greatest enemy.

As an advocate of a strength-based model of psychology, I am insatiably curious about choice, consequences, and self-worth. It is the seemingly insignificant choices we make, every single moment of every waking day, that sets the tone for our lives. Whenever I am working with a client, I am keen to explore their choices, as it gives me invaluable access to a person's sense of self-worth. I often witness people making decisions out of fear, or based on a fantasy of how things should be. Often, they ignore their gut instincts and by-pass the red-flag signs. This frequently results in further problems and again shines a spotlight that illuminates a person's self-worth.

The truth is, people seldom believe in their own worth. I recently asked a client whether her decision to stay in a lacklustre job was an act of self-love or self-hate. There is no judgement. I have a curious mind and want to understand her decision-making process. Most importantly I want to understand what purpose it is serving for her, to stay in a bleak situation. There is always a pay-off, even when we screw ourselves over: at some level, a need of some sort is being met. Often, fear is a driving, conniving factor influencing the process. The amount of resistance that I encounter helps me to gain an insight into how much (or little) a person values themselves. Our choices provide a wealth of information. When we are not aware of our motives, we unknowingly sell ourselves short. We play small. We tolerate nonsense. We live in hopeless hope. We live in our fantasies and, rather than face reality, we distort, deny or contort it, causing ourselves immense pain. I ask the heartbroken, dumped, used and abused 32-year-old woman sitting before me: are you hurting yourself by getting back with 'won't commit Fred'? Is your decision an act of self-love or self-sabotage? Only she can decide, and only she can truly know the answer. **The greatest battle is always within.**

Through the window of our seemingly insignificant choices, gold is revealed. This gives me, the therapist, wide-ranging insights into the value each person places upon their existence. As my clients reveal the tapestry of their lives, I get to understand their self-worth in action and the benefits to them of selling themselves short. Yes: the benefits. It is fundamental that I unearth the benefits of playing small, because our self-sabotaging behaviours often serve a purpose. In my view, and many scholars would agree, we are the ultimate creators of our reality. If this is true, then it naturally follows that we have the power to change that reality. We have the power not only to create our misery but also to heal ourselves. In the end, it all comes down to choice.

The view that our choices create our reality may seem controversial, airy-fairy or even woo-woo. This way of looking at human distress flies in the face of the medical view, that we have 'deficit brains', in need of ever more medication to restore balance and harmony. While medication may well have its place in a time of crisis, more and more frequently, my private clients seek me out as an alternative. They're uncomfortable with the idea of 'popping pills' and not dealing with the root cause of their problems, and so my practice grows. Meanwhile, the government's drive to raise 'mental health' awareness, is accompanied by the cutting of services, increased wait times, and shoe-horning people into generic CBT group programmes. It's absurd and incredibly unfair. The glaring void, it always strikes me, is that nobody is talking about the qualities that make for a great, fulfilled and wholesome life.

In the presence of most mental health problems, there will, to varying degrees, be an absence of what I describe as the key qualities for a great life. These are: **self-love, self-responsibility, self-acceptance, self-compassion, self-awareness, personal power, authenticity.** All of these combine to provide a person with **a sense of purpose.** If such qualities are absent - to one degree or another - in someone's life, then I can predict, with near-certainty, that sadness will follow. And this is a truth that has far-reaching repercussions, for us as individuals and as members of a society where mental health conditions are rising rapidly, affecting younger people at epidemic rates. What has gone so terribly wrong? That larger question is beyond the scope of the present book. It is, however, an absolute crying shame that more attention is not given to the qualities that make for a fulfilled life. The qualities that I endeavor to live by, and it is this glaring void that has inspired me to write this book.

WHAT IS SELF-LOVE AND WHY IS IT THE KEY?

Self-love is the bedrock for a fulfilled, wholesome life. It is essential if we want to unlock our potential and become our greatest selves. An absence of self-love will shrivel the human spirit and, when our spirit is shrivelled, common mental health problems will take root. I would say that self-love is an action. While some activities can easily be classified as such – for example, attending spas or going to the gym – other actions will be unique to us as individuals, and to the personal challenges that we are encountering. There will be times when it is an act of self-love to cut people out of our lives in spite of our feelings – some folks are just not good for us. Personally, I regard having a cleaner as an act of self-love, as well as leaving toxic WhatsApp groups or blocking emotionally unavailable men from my phone. For me, personally, all these activities represent self-love in action. It is my responsibility to protect my vulnerability in the best way that I can. So what about you? Who has your best interests at heart?

Ultimately, we teach others how to treat us, and the starting-point is always how much we believe **we are worth**. Self-love influences all aspects of our lives - from work, to mate choices, to how we deal with life's problems. It is complemented by qualities such as **self-appreciation** (bigging ourselves up), **self-preservation** (looking after our own best interests), and **self-compassion**. Self-love, being kind to ourselves, is a **key for a great, fulfilled, wholesome life**. Its absence will often become most noticeable in our intimate relationships. If self-love is compromised over a prolonged period of time, sadness will take a hold, and we are likely as well to be vulnerable to abuse. When we do not like, and maybe even hate, the person that we are, life just gets harder. In stark contrast to L'Oreal's ad campaign, 'Because you're worth it', a life devoid of self-love says, 'You're not worth it'. In addition, you will be prone to developing the kind of damaging behaviours that will keep you in a vicious, grid-locked cycle: behaviours such as **poor personal boundaries**, **people-pleasing, putting others on pedestals, denial, and avoidance**.

As the years go by, life will hurt more and more if self-defeating behaviours become entrenched. It's also likely that people will use and abuse you - take advantage of you and use you for their own gains. Additionally, when you fail to incorporate self-love into your life in a meaningful practical way, you will be incredibly grateful for crumbs of (perceived) love, a modicum of validation and superficial reassurance that any-old-body loves you. After all, you don't even like yourself (let alone love yourself). The mere fact that someone will claim to love you will be immense. I will be so bold as to suggest that you will cling to that person, even in the face of considerable disrespect. In fact, you will bend over backwards, like a gymnast, to accommodate them. Mariah Carey sang 'I can't live, if living is without you' in her cover of Harry Nilsson's song 'Without You'. When you hate yourself, life may well seem intolerable if that person threatens to abandon you. In fact, when you fail to love yourself, your susceptibility to nonsense and ill-treatment will be high, as will the chances that desperation will set in, too. This type of behaviour is likely to play out most vividly in intimate relationships. At some level, you do not believe that you are worthy of good treatment and end up accepting whatever you get. As time passes, you will probably become accustomed to the pain, but there may be a fighting spirit within you that - even if infrequently - whispers, 'you can do better'. If the person you adore doesn't walk out on you, then they may take you to the brink. This may be the brink of despair - or the brink of 'I'm not going to take this any more'.

My sincere hope is that one day, all that pain will inspire you to change.

Without self-love, we are vulnerable to abuse, neglect, and a multitude of violations. Without self-love, we are susceptible to 'other-love'. We will adore, worship and idolise other people. When we put others on pedestals, it really is not good for us. We dehumanise them, ignore the red flags, and make them god-like figures. Invariably, this type of behaviour indicates that we are looking outside of ourselves for validation. Therefore, we do not trust in ourselves or our decisions, and we will look to others to give us the 'thumbs up'. When we do not trust in ourselves, our decision-making processes are vulnerable. We will be heavily dependent on the judgement and opinions of key people, as we need their permission and approval before we make a move. When our validation comes exclusively from outside sources, our personal power will be diminished, because ultimately we are trusting in others and not in ourselves.

In addition, if we don't learn to 'big ourselves up', then we are likely to 'put ourselves down'. In fact, we often do this without even noticing it. When working with my clients, I pay close attention to subtle 'put downs', and I challenge where this thinking comes from. I ask, 'what other nasty names do you call yourself?' The fact of the matter is this: if we hate the skin we're in, and loathe who we are, then we will be highly dependent on others for the 'thumbs up'. We'll depend on them for a measure of our worth. The greatest issue with this is that humans are fickle and often change their minds. When they no longer love us, want us, like us, or need us, then we are on the scrap heap and as such we are incredibly vulnerable. Why? Because we do not rate *ourselves*! Our framework for validation is exclusively outside of ourselves. We needed the other person far more than they needed us. This is often why it is so catastrophic when intimate relationships break down. We are literally watching our entire self-esteem walk out the door - as Mariah Carey sings, 'I can't live, if living is without you'.

This does not mean that break-ups are easy for self-loving people. Of course it hurts when their relationships fall apart, but they have a self-validating core that sustains them through adversity. The fall is hard, but not as devastating as it is for someone who self-loathes. There is just no getting away from it: life is difficult. Developing the key qualities for a great life provides a buffer, the resources that encourage us to look within, to take responsibility, to trust in ourselves and to give ourselves permission to do whatever we need to do. It may not sound dramatic, but these simple qualities can make all the difference for us through the inevitable trials and tribulations of life.

So, **self-love - or self-hate? It's for you to decide**. The two coexist much like everything else on planet earth. The world operates in opposites: night - day, light - dark, happy - sad, up - down, male - female. You cannot have one without the other. The absence of self-love results in self-hatred and if self-hatred predominantly governs your life, life will be grim. Prolonged self-hatred leads to depression and, if left unchecked, depression can lead to hopelessness. Hopelessness and suicide have a strong correlation - it is important that we are acutely aware of these bleak facts. Let's not avoid it. **The truth will always set us free**. As ever, **self-awareness is the key** and the more aware we can be, the more we can make informed and conscious choices. **Remember, even if we decide not to decide, we are still making a decision.** Annoyingly, this does not always mean we will like the choices available to us. At times, none of our options will delight us, but when we fail to decide, our personal power will be compromised.

I cannot overstate how important personal power is for our wellbeing; and it is especially crucial when making choices. Personal power is linked to autonomy (self-rule), so when we lose that power we become like sheep, led by something outside of ourselves. A lack of personal power is another contributory factor that hinders personal greatness and feeds into anxiety and depression. When we lose our autonomy, we lose ourselves: we become robotic and our humanity is slowly eroded. It is inevitable, then, that our happiness will also slip away. Show me any abusive or toxic relationship and I will show you a person who has diminished autonomy and personal power. The two go hand in hand. It's as simple as that.

GET WOKE: SELF-AWARENESS IS NO JOKE

Getting WOKE (to quote Jim Carrey) is like being in the film The Matrix and taking the red pill. We get a growing understanding of what's really going on, and find out that we were wrong about much of what we understood to be truth. When we make a conscious decision to become our greatest self, self-awareness will be fundamental to our quest for a more fulfilled life. There are no short cuts when it comes to developing self-insight. It is a process and it takes time. We are building a relationship with ourselves here, so please be patient and kind. The more self-aware we are, the more we can make informed and conscious choices. When we make informed, conscious, decisions we no longer subscribe to the notion of 'oh, it just happened'. Ugh-Ugh: those days are long gone. In The Matrix, Morpheus offers Neo the red or the blue pill. For me, the blue pill represents being in a sleep where we believe things just happen to us – ignorant bliss, if you like. Whereas the red pill opens our eyes and stimulates our critical thinking, so that we begin to see dynamics at a deeper level – spiritual, even.

Taking the red pill is where we start to get real and raw with ourselves, and increasingly curious about how we contributed to the calamity that causes us stress. We become like Inspector Morse, only this time, we are looking within. The more we grow in awareness, the more we see the bigger picture and the deeper intentions behind our actions. It becomes much harder to lie to ourselves when we take the red pill: our eyes are wide open and, as time goes by, we give up even bothering to try. We know it's pointless. Instead, we get curious about ourselves. Finally, we start to see the writing that has always been on the wall.

When you make it your mission to become more self-aware, you also start to get curious about the rationale that underlies your decisions. Over time, if you are dedicated to the process, you should start to shift towards making informed choices, where you are hyper-alert to the potential benefits and drawbacks of a given situation. As a therapist, my part in this profound process is to help you understand what is being unfurled and to be a confidante that shows you your truth. In due course, I reveal to my clients their unhelpful patterns and self-sabotaging behaviours that keep them stuck in vicious cycles. Let's take Amanda, for example. She was a driven self-made marketer with a busy consultancy. She knew she had a gift for inspiring people, she knew she could play bigger, yet, day in and day out, she would distract herself with low-level activities, reading emails, creating social media posts and having idle, saccharine chit-chat with sweet-talk guys who were never really up to standard.

Six months after our first consultation, Amanda is 'woke' and very much conscious that she is idling her time away. She knows that she is avoiding doing the work she needs to do, if she is to show up in a bigger way in the world. But for now, it is her choice to play small and that is absolutely ok. Through therapy, we have come to understand the underlying reason for her self-sabotaging ways – a deep-seated fear of stepping up and standing out. In standing out, she fears she will become a target for haters and backbiters. She has a fear of success. Bigger success will take her into the unknown and out of her comfort zone. Now, when Amanda gets embroiled in idle chit-chat, or any other kind of procrastination, she knows exactly what she is doing, and what she is avoiding. She is awakened and, while she still procrastinates, she understands the purpose that this behaviour serves. Believe it or not, this type of conscious insight is empowering. Why? Because now she is aware, and is free to make different choices. Idle chit-chat, or write her book? Does she take a step closer to growing her business, or get caught in low-level day-to-day tasks? Only she can decide, and the choice is always hers.

As Amanda and I continue to grow in our therapeutic relationship, we are exploring the reasons behind her fear. My ambition is for her to see for herself how and (most importantly) why she sells herself short, settles for less and screws herself over. Together, as our relationship deepens, we unknit decades of experience that have shaped her identity. I pay close attention to nonverbal cues: changes in breath, eye wetness and tone. The body is such a truth-teller, and truth has a beautiful way of seeping out. It's a profound experience to co-create and to witness. Amanda no longer needs to justify why she plays small. The veil has been lifted. The red pill is in full effect. She is free to decide what to do, and to make decisions in truth and full awareness. Together, we are on an excavation mission, digging down deeper to explore and unearth the more entrenched, stubborn, fear-based behaviour that hinders her from fully stepping into her greatness.

Humans are incredibly complicated beings. At times, we can be our own worst enemy. When we are not fully prepared to act in self-love, then self-sabotaging behaviours will naturally ensue. What's interesting is that, if we are defensive and stubborn, then it is an indicator that there must be an important benefit that keeps us stuck in a self-destructive loop. I make it my personal ambition to explore and understand why this behaviour continues in spite of our knowing better. Conscious self-sabotage indicates some type of buried fear or an unreadiness to let go of unhelpful behaviour. As long as the client is willing, I feel a duty to understand why there is a vast discrepancy between behaviour and knowledge. Once these insights are revealed, we can inspect them, hold them up to the light, and check the sell-by date. We can understand that some of our unhelpful behaviours are redundant coping strategies. They served us well in the past, but today they hinder our progress.

In the main, self-awareness promotes self-responsibility. As a result, our ability to blame others will be limited when we begin to truly see how we 'screw ourselves over'. Additionally, we may start to make **well-informed** and **thought-through** decisions. This is especially important for complicated, delicate issues. If we can slow down enough, rather than just spontaneously reacting in a knee-jerk fashion, we get access to our inner dialogue, and this is gold. Now, if we pay close attention, we hear the inner voice that influences our behaviour; we begin to notice what we say to ourselves and how we justify our actions. In this split second, as we notice the chatter in our minds, we give ourselves a beautiful opportunity to 'notice what we notice'. More gold. In this stimulus gap, we give ourselves a space to observe our reactions. Absolute platinum gold. It is essential to this process that we are incredibly truthful with ourselves: denial is a threat to self-responsibility. As we become increasingly real with ourselves, we will develop a heightened awareness of the potential consequences of a given action.

Take Bob, for example. Rather than acting blindly and not understanding how Narcissistic Nancy hurt him for the 200th time, he now knows that, if he decides to unblock her from his phone, then he has made a choice to re-open communication. Once unblocked, if he finds himself being manipulated and controlled by his ex once again, Bob - now awakened - knows that he co-created the situation. Therefore, he is not a victim. It is not Nancy's fault. She will do what she does. People are often consistent and she has the right to live her life as she sees fit. Bob has choices too: he can decide to stay or leave. If he decides to stay, then he should be encouraged to accept Nancy as she is, because that is ultimately what he is going to get. As ever, the choice is up to him. I respect free will.

In the end, when we grow in our self-awareness, there is no pretending, its becomes harder and harder to lie to ourselves. We get clear and real with ourselves first. That way, we can see and understand how we contribute to and create our own misery. True self-awareness is where we are fully aware of the benefits and limitations of a given situation. Moving forward, if Bob wants to reconnect with Nancy then he does so mindfully, knowing full well **prior** to the situation that his emotional needs will not be met and that she is highly likely to manipulate and control him. His eyes are wide open to reality, which is in stark contrast to when he was in the dark and unaware. When we are unaware, we are living in 'ignorant bliss'. We are visionless and believe things just 'happen' to us. We take little or no responsibility, and the blame belongs to others.

When we steer our behaviour in ways where we are real and raw with ourselves, there is a lessening of our need to distort, deny or minimise the consequences of a situation. Our eyes are wide open, and we take off our rose-coloured spectacles. We accord full weight to the potential drawbacks as well as the benefits of our decisions. The advantage of this way of behaving is that we know full well what we are getting into. Therefore, we cannot blame anyone else when it goes wrong. This truth can be uncomfortable, especially in therapy, where it can evoke resistance, frustration, denial, over-long explanations, and justifications. Radical self-responsibility is not for the faint-hearted, and people do not necessarily like it. They like the idea of responsibility, but not the reality. As such, when we get too close to a nerve on our therapeutic journey, defence mechanisms kick in. Generally speaking, people tend to like consistency so that, while they have the ambition to change and the option is always open to them, they are not always prepared to make the sacrifices that are required. They want change, they desire change but, when the going gets tough, the ripples and consequences are perceived as being too disruptive -

and so they retreat or stop short.

The question that fascinates me is, how long will self-sabotage continue? The truth is, it will roll on for as long as it serves a purpose. As bizarre as it may seem, I try to elicit from my clients the benefits of being stuck. Why? Because if we desire radical change, we will encounter a raft of unintended consequences that may become an obstacle to that change. You see, when the majority of our lives are built upon our 'selling ourselves short', it will get prickly when we start to change, and I wholeheartedly respect people's reasons for only taking it so far. The beauty and simplicity of self-awareness is that we create our reality by our choices: if we don't like a situation, we have the power to change it. Easier said than done, right? Well, while such a statement may seem airy fairy, it really is that simple. Yet simplicity is often underrated.

In the main, what tends to happen is that we need to go on repeating vicious cycles until it becomes a bore, it hurts too much, or we hit our personal rock bottom. At this point, the pain kick-starts serious self-reflection, questioning and, most importantly, meaningful action. The same ol', same ol' no longer works and we would rather risk change than wither and die in sameness. We want out! The wheels are about to be set in motion. **Remember, we create our reality by the small choices that we make each day.** We often create our pain, we screw ourselves over, sell ourselves short, and have the audacity to blame others - when we co-created the very situation that hurts. We ignored the warning signs, lied to ourselves and distorted reality for a fantasy we have in our minds. We live in hope, yet it's hopeless hope and we end up making ourselves ill. People seem to struggle to accept this truth as reality, and some get annoyed and defensive. However, I find it rather freeing to know that if I create my misery, then I am also at liberty to change it. Is that not a gift? We have the power! People who are resistant to this truth like to believe that things happen to them. They don't think they play a part, and miss all the small nuanced decisions and behaviours of their own that have brought about their pain and suffering. Is ignorance really bliss? Well, I don't think so, but it does have its benefits.

WANTS AND NEEDS: KNOW THE DIFFERENCE

Self-love is a continuous endeavour, and we must be kind to ourselves when we fall short. Falling short is inevitable. There are no hard and fast rules. Self-love is a practice, like flossing your teeth: we all know we should do it, but don't always make the effort. Such is life. Remember, high doses of judgement and condemnation will take their toll on our spirit, and this situation is worse when the criticism continuously comes from ourselves: we have nowhere to run. The antidote is to develop self-compassion, an antidote that is filled with kindness and understanding, the very same qualities that we give away in abundance to others. Developing this practice is especially important if we are actively pursuing personal greatness.

With that said, it is wise to know that, when life's pinch turns into a punch, then often (not always) an absence of self-love is fuelling the process. What we need is not what we want, and what we want is not what we often need. Knowing the difference is incredibly important. Sometimes we will have to defy our urges and go against the well-worn grain. At the same time, self-awareness is the key that will assist us in navigating life's tumultuous seas. **Remember, you will not always like the choices you will have to make when you actively practise self-love**. When changing any behaviour, it can be helpful to compare it to breaking in a new pair of shoes: it is uncomfortable at first, and it takes time to break in, but when it does, new behaviour becomes the norm and in time becomes comfortable.

Let's take Maggie as an example: on a ten-day Caribbean cruise she met Richard, who appeared to value and appreciate her quirky style. Maggie fell hard and fast for him, and thought that she had found her 'soul mate'. She desperately **wanted** Richard to be 'the one', and all the signs indicated that he felt the same way too. Utter synergy. There was so much to be excited about. In spite of meeting in the Caribbean, Richard lived locally in London. Like Maggie, he already had two children, and he was a well-established professional. They had a magical, intense connection, and shared the same sense of humour. It just couldn't get any better.

Maggie thought that she **needed** Richard, and she was desperate to settle down and build a new life. She would have married him in a heartbeat. All he had to do was to ask. However, within six weeks of coming home, Richard began to withdraw. He became difficult to get hold of, he did not return calls, and trying to pin him down for a date was impossible. Eventually, he agreed to meet her, two months in advance. He said that it was the only time he had available. Did she want to take it? Maggie agreed, but she felt uncomfortable. She was devastated and profoundly embarrassed about the way her relationship had nose-dived: she had shouted about her new-found love from the rooftops and now she felt like a fool. How could she have gotten it so wrong again? She held out for Richard, avoided talking about him to friends, and acted as if it was no big deal. But it hurt. When he rang she became anxious, and sweat broke out on her brow. She struggled to be herself and, as he was so prickly, she had to choose her words carefully otherwise she would offend him and then he would not talk to her for weeks. She loved him, but just did not understand how she had lost her voice. For some strange reason, he was difficult and she could not challenge him. How had it come to this?

Maggie knew she had to confront Richard, but his tricky ways made that hard to do, and she feared she would be dumped. She felt shame and humiliation, as if she had been played. Richard had such a clever way of deflecting conversation, and nothing was ever his fault. She thought she **needed** Richard, but she actually **wanted** him and there is a stark difference. We often get this one confused: a need is described as something we must have to survive. Maggie did not need Richard to survive. She kept silent and optimistic, and put up with his nonsense for over a year. She spent that year wondering if the problem was him or her. But as much as she tried to accommodate him, she always missed the mark and ended up causing offence and being reprimanded. Maggie noticed her increased anxiety in the lead-up to a date: he was always late, and always had an epic excuse. At their final meeting, Maggie waited over an hour, and realised during that hour that if she continued a relationship with Richard, then anxiety, despair, disrespect and second-guessing herself would be a frequent occurrence. She asked herself one question: am I willing to put up with this?

The writing is often on the wall, but we refuse to read it. Maggie realised, in that hour, that she had to make a choice, either to accept or reject the relationship. It really is as simple as that! Maggie was making an important decision: did she honour her supposed 'need' for a relationship, knowing there was a high emotional toll? Or did she batten down the hatches, weather the storm, and practise self-love, self-care and self-regard? Honouring herself would mean the demise of a relationship that she so desperately thought she **needed**. She heard that little fear-based inner voice whisper: 'What if you don't meet anyone again? It's been five years since your last relationship.' She acknowledged that voice, but the pain of holding on and being 'hopeful' became way too much to bear. The crux of the matter was whether she honoured her **needs** and **wants**: knowing the difference is incredibly important.

Maggie decided to let Richard know her truth and, as expected, their relationship ended. Interestingly, some five years on, Maggie still has feelings for him. Love is a little odd like that! In spite of still loving him, Maggie makes wise choices rather than purely emotional ones. Initially, she blocked his number, texted him instead of using WhatsApp (no two-blue-tick anxiety). She un-followed and unfriended him too, as well as removing him from all other social media platforms. This may not sound like drastic action, but it is an important act of self-preservation and a sign of self-love. Maggie is not in denial about her feelings for Richard: she still annoyingly carries a torch for him, but she knows he is not good for her and as such has decided to cut all ties and has em-ployed a no-contact rule.

From time to time their paths cross, and naturally she still feels a pull towards him. Richard's a charmer and knows Maggie well. They still have a bond. But Maggie is no fool, she exercises wis-dom and keeps it moving. **Temptation is better to avoid, than to resist.** She knows that if she wants to reignite their relation-ship, she can do it with ease, but she knows exactly what she will get: a 'wham-bam thank you mam' set-up, and she now believes she's worthy of much more than that. Maggie is mindful of how easy it is to get swept back into an unhealthy relationship. This situation mirrors her strained relationship with her father, so she must be cautious. Let's remember, people: having a bond does not necessarily mean that a wholesome and fulfilling relationship will naturally follow. Many folks get this one confused and hold on with valiant hope that a toxic relationship will some day come good, while all the time there is a drip-drip effect, chipping away at their self-esteem. Having a connection is a great founda-tion for a relationship, but other qualities need to co-exist, qual-ities such as respectfulness, integrity, reciprocity, sensitivity and trust. Without these qualities, a bond could keep you in bondage.

Human needs and wants are terms that people often confuse. Maggie was upset that her relationship with Richard ended. She openly expressed that she **needed** Richard in her life. But in the end, she knew that Richard came at a high emotional price, and her wellbeing would be compromised if she stayed with him. Maggie did not **need** Richard to survive. Richard was a **want.** He was not essential to her life. Knowing this subtle difference can be helpful and, if we are mindful, can aid us in letting go, quicker and faster, of people who are not good for us. Acting in such ways may seem radical, yet it is a clear sign of practising self-love. When we begin to absorb self-loving principles into our lives, we reduce the damage that can be done by people who do not have our best interests at heart. We are declaring our worthiness and acting in accordance with that belief!

Declare your worthiness, yes! But, we must act in accordance wih our beliefs.

BREAKING CYCLES

Pattern recognition may not sound like a natural term to comple-ment self-love, but it really is. Noticing our relationship patterns is essential to self-love. When our patterns of relating become explicit to us, we are on the road to becoming increasingly em-powered. We are no longer blind about our decisions and, in time, we can start to make different choices. For example, if you are a perpetual giver you're highly likely to attract takers. So if you're fed up with people taking your kindness for weakness, then being self-aware is essential. You will begin to notice how you co-create situations where needy people feed from you. Remember, there are no quick fixes here, you have to be patient with yourself and notice what you notice. One simple way to break this cycle would be to stop giving. How easy is that? Easier said than done. Another option is to articulate your needs to others. See what happens, experiment with life. If you are a giver, then it is likely that people don't consider your needs. In the first instance, start-ing to articulate your needs will probably be agonising, but trust me, it will be good for you in the long run.

It's so important to experience difference: see how it feels, try it for size and notice how people respond to you. The ideas above are shining examples of how to break well-grooved patterns. Self-awareness provides us with choice, and we break patterns by making different decisions. Now, this new way of being will be a challenge and will take some practice. We should keep in mind the analogy with breaking in a new pair of shoes. Being kind to ourselves is essential. **Self-love is the key,** and the more aware we are of our patterns, the more we can empower ourselves via our choices. The situations where we are most challenged are also of the most interest here: these are the scenarios where we are most likely to resort to old habits, and these habits are the hardest and most stubborn to remove.

Remember, the most important relationship we have is with ourselves. I know, you have heard it a hundred times and it's a bore if you really don't get it. But it is the absolute truth. I hasten to add, though, that we can only meet ourselves in relationship with others. The adage goes, **show me your friends and I will show you who you are**. This saying is gold. It is the people with whom we surround ourselves who reveal our self-worth or lack of it. What frustrates us about a relationship is the very area of our lives to which we must pay careful attention. Relationships provide us with a window into our self-worth, one that illuminates the areas that we may need to work on. It is when we rub up against, interact with, and come into contact with others, that we come face to face with our internal world. The aspects of ourselves that we discover through other people could not be revealed in isolation. Therefore relationships are of paramount importance when it comes to understanding who we are and who we are becoming. We often project our needs and wants on to others, and the key to healthy, wholesome relationships is to offer to ourselves what we have projected on to others. That way, we are empowered and, when someone comes along offering us less than we would give to ourselves, we unmistakably know that we're settling for less if we engage in such a relationship.

Take Kelly, for example: she often found herself drawn to narcissistic and selfish men. Over the years she became more aware of her relationship patterns and her pull to emotionally unavailable men. Kelly believed she wanted to be in a committed relationship. However, she spent much time pursuing the 'Won't commit Freds' of this world. Rather interestingly, she would ridicule decent men as boring or 'too keen'. 'There's just no excitement, Keeley', she would tell me. It appeared that Kelly was rejecting and chastising the very men who had the potential to offer her what she wanted. She was caught in a vicious cycle, a cycle that said more about her self-worth than it did about the men she was drawn to.

Through therapy she came to realise that she was so used to settling for less, that getting what she wanted frightened her. Interestingly, committed, decent, loyal men were a threat to her, as she had no blueprint for relating to them. Plus, life was predictable with the 'Won't commit Freds', and a safe guy took her out of her comfort zone. The relationships she chose hurt Kelly, but it was a familiar kind of pain, a pain that stretched back to her early years, and had been replicated throughout her adult life - the pain of inconsistent and unsafe love. She felt safe within the restricted confines of unhealthy relationships. Bizarrely, dating a 'safe guy' made her vulnerable. She had no previous experience, and such men never really stood a chance as she chastised, ridiculed and put them down. The nub of the issue was that she regarded kind considerate men as simply weak, and they actually repulsed her.

Kelly was far more comfortable with the highs and lows of narcissistic relationships. This was her norm, and mirrored her difficult relationship with her father. When she decided to explore a relationship with Steady Eddie (a man who wanted to commit), Kelly soon realised the small and nuanced ways in which she pushed him away. She chastised, found fault, called him names like boring, dull: 'Keeley, he's just got no va-va-voom.' Ultimately, Steady Eddie did not have a hope because of her unconscious prejudice and discrimination. Through therapy, she came to realise how her problematic relationship with her father was at the core, and that at some level she was recreating her pain though her relationships with emotionally unavailable men. She truly believed that she wanted to be in a loving relationship. In reality, however, she was rejecting the men that could offer her the very thing she desired. The irony is that what she wanted, she could never have with 'Won't commit Fred'. Such relationships are all about the chase: when they catch you, they devour your flesh, while at the same time eyeing up the next piece of prey.

Together we explored what Jung described as the dark side of Kelly's personality. This process required her to be open, non-defensive and brutally honest as we delved into her life at a deeper level. We extracted gold in those sessions, and came to understand why men's kindness repulsed her and why having what she wanted made her freeze. Over time, she began to steer her ship in different directions, pushing through her own resistance and fears. This was not easy, but neither was being stuck. Kelly has reached a new plateau and witnesses new horizons, and finally feels ready to give the Steady Eddies of this world a chance. She has moved beyond her prejudices and wants to connect with someone genuine, considerate and attentive. Kindness is not totally comfortable for her, but it no longer repulses her in the same way. Plus, she understands her patterns, and is empowered to make different choices. 'It's such a refreshing experience, Keeley.' Now that she is 'woke', our sessions have reached a natural end. Kelly has come to realise that receiving safe, consistent love is one of her greatest challenges, and she embraces that challenge with all her might.

THE ROAD TO SELF-LOVE

We cannot truly understand the concept of self-love until we have pushed through our defences and practised it in a meaningful way. This may come as bad news for my head-over-heart thinkers, but it's the truth. Self-love is learnt experientially, and knowing it from head knowledge alone is not sufficient. Self-love needs to be practised. That way, we assimilate knowledge into behaviour, and it is through this process that we start to exercise wisdom. This is when we come to truly see the glory of self-love's revolutionary and transformative power. However, moving from understanding to actually integrating self-love practices into our lives is the tricky part. I won't lie: when it comes to changing ingrained self-deprecating habits, it takes time and patience to retrain ourselves. We are endeavouring to create new normals here, new ways of being, new pathways in our brains, so do take it easy on yourself. This is especially difficult for all those perfectionists out there, who castigate themselves for the slightest of slip-ups. This is not a pass or fail exam: it's life. Be kind. Be considerate. Be compassionate. Self-brutality is not going to be useful to you.

We learn, then, to love ourselves through experience – through the abundance of opportunities that come our way for us to practise, and to try and try again. We can stay stuck, we can coast, or we can grow. The choice is ours, and we can be comforted knowing that there is always another chance. Now of course, if you are a perfectionist, or someone that needs to be in total control all the time, then the notion of experiential, 'let's trust the process' learning may not delight you. There are no hard-and-fast rules, no scripts to follow, and you don't know what may come at you. But take heart, there is incredible power in letting go and trusting uncertainty. I find it heart-warming that each moment of every waking day provides me with a chance to try again to act in self-loving ways. Trust the process. All things can work for your good, if you are woke!

Self-love is a journey. There are no quick fixes but, as long as you are breathing, opportunities will flow. So how do you begin to bring self-love into your life in a meaningful way? Well, firstly, beware of anyone telling you that self-love can be achieved in a few easy steps, like 1,2,3 or Do-Re-Mi. Humans are far more complex than that, and defying well-worn habits is hard and takes conscious effort. Good therapy will assist you, and group therapy has the potential to speed up the process of self-awareness. Make self-love a life's mission, a continuous practice and endeavour. At times, self-love will feel like a slow crawl; at others, like total stagnation; and heck, sometimes you will feel like you are in reverse. But it's all good. Stay woke. Everything is material, and potent life lessons can be gleaned from the harshest of negative experiences.

The secret is to remain conscious. Even when you are screwing yourself over, observe your behaviour, observe how you are pulled to non-progressiveness. There is value in these experiences too. Notice what you notice. Get a book, make notes, document the small and subtle ways in which you sell yourself short. Believe it or not, but this is gold too. Why? Because you are getting unadulterated access to your inner self-saboteur, an aspect of yourself that I call 'Cruella de Vil (an evil, wicked and cruel antagonist from the Disney film, *The Hundred and One Dalmatians*). When you know that you are putting yourself in situations that no longer serve you, ask yourself this set of questions:

1. What need is being met?

2. What do I get out of this experience?

3. If I were to let go, what am I scared of?

Note down your answers. This information is priceless: you are exposing the enemy within. Remember, there are no short cuts or cheat sheets. Self-love is not a sprint. Self-love is a process, an experiential process. No one ever arrives at a final destination I'm afraid to you. However, the wonderful news is it's a perpetual state of becoming, learning and **self-awareness is key**. So stay woke, people. Get still, do yoga, try meditation. Try something different. Reconnect with the passions from the past. Do more of what makes your heart sing. Give yourself permission. Stop delaying. Say yes, practise saying no, and connect to an inner wisdom that is available to all of us if we can yank ourselves away from our smart phones.

Remember, there is wisdom within and you know much more than you think. The thinking, logical head is riddled with limitations, so get inquisitive about your thoughts. You don't always have to believe what you think. Observe your thoughts. Practise mindfulness. The answers are always within. The ultimate power lies in our choices. Therefore it is important that we pause, before we react. When we pause, we create a gap. In neuro-linguistic programming, this action is called a stimulus gap. In such moments, we are giving ourselves a massive opportunity to disrupt our unhelpful default settings. By pausing and paying close attention, we will hear the whisper and directional force of our inner dialogue. For example, I am sitting here in Cafe Nero, writing this book. When I ordered a coffee, instantly I wanted a cake and began eyeing up the calorific treats. I paused. I asked myself: 'Do you really need a cake? Did you not go to the gym this morning, Keeley?' In that stimulus gap, I created a small window to question my actions. In that gap, we bless ourselves with an opportunity to respond from a more empowered, considered place and, in doing so, we create a golden opportunity to override well-worn impulsive behaviours. I am happy to say that I did not buy the cake. While this example may not seem like a high-pressured, life-or-death situation, I encourage you to 'sweat the small stuff'. By the time you get to an extreme situation, where every fibre of your being is tested, you will have built new mind-muscles and gifted yourself with a new way to respond to the world. You really are a badass.

◆ ◆ ◆

On your new-found self-love expedition, it is inevitable that you will backslide, cock things up, get it wrong and fall back into situations, places and people that no longer serve you. That's a given: expect it, embrace it. You are equipping yourself with valuable insights here. Pay close attention to what you notice. The insights are gold. This is especially important if you know that you are deliberately selling yourself short. Or if you are entertaining people who cannot elevate you or who, at worst, bring you down, there is often a deep-seated fear underpinning the process. Usually it's unworthiness. Unworthiness is a bugger and a master of disguise. Just like a stubborn splinter buried in the depths of your big toe, unworthiness needs to be prised out, exposed and inspected, so you can marvel at it and then flick it into oblivion. However, unlike the flickable splinter, unworthiness finds ways of morphing. It's elusive, a chameleon, and has a habit of submerging and re-emerging in a different guise, in a different form, at a different time. I jest not when I say that the greatest battle is within.

Needless to say, you have to be kind to yourself when, as is to be expected, you backslide. Being kind to yourself, even when you 'fail' or repeat negative patterns, will help give you an opportunity to develop **self-compassion**, another key quality for a great life. **Remember, there is no failure, only feedback**. At times you will fall short, at other times you will **screw yourself over**. Getting to know the enemy within is an integral part of the process. The highs, the absolute lows, the joy, the pain and the suffering: all these are essential elements for a great, fulfilled life. We cannot have light without darkness. Many life-changing lessons can be gleaned from the shadowy places in the valleys of life.

It may seem odd, but I appreciate the sting that adversity brings. That sharpness focuses the mind, separates the wheat from the chaff, and brings clarity with a chiming 'BING'. Adversity is where we re-evaluate, eradicate, and get acute focus on what matters and what really doesn't. I think of Amy Winehouse, and Adele, who poured their pain into song, to find massive stardom because their heartfelt anguish chimed with a pain of our own. Those artists channelled their pain into a creative outlet that raised the hairs on the back of our necks and moved untold listeners to tears. Is that not the sweetest of victories? Adversity harnessed mindfully can revolutionise the course of one's life and in doing so can unexpectedly enhance the lives of others. That is one of the wonderful secrets to life.

The key really is about how we respond and react to the adverse condition. I respect that for many people the notion that good can come out of hellish personal experiences may be nothing short of infuriating. This is especially true when you are in your darkest depths of despair, and life has flipped 360 degrees through no fault of your own. I have no ambition to minimise or discount the degree of hurt or devastation that you are going through. It's unfair and sometimes we are dealt the meanest of hands. But **time is the greatest healer and time reveals all**. As inconvenient as this truth may seem, good can come from bad and good can come from evil. We either let the situation define us, and let it eat us up from the inside out, or we harness our hardship and radically revolutionise and re-define who we are because of it. We start a cause, join a support group or create one if it does not exist, give a helping hand to someone else going through the same anguish. But just don't give up and don't give in, I implore you.

Grieve if you need to grieve, cry if you need to cry. Get sad if you need to be sad. Do what you need to do. I tell you: your greatest victories can come from the hardest of adversities. Just google the following people that I admire to get a glimpse of the life I am trying to describe: Rollin Funky, lifestyle blogger; Clara Holmes; Jennifer Hudson, singer; Nick Vujicic, motivational speaker; Les Brown, author and speaker. If we can summon up the courage, conviction and strength from deep down within us, we may be blessed enough to discover that there is a mighty reservoir inside that we had no idea existed (listen to Whitney Houston's 'I Didn't Know My Own Strength' for inspiration). If we can access that pool of power, we may be one of the lucky few who harness devasting experiences to inspire and encourage others. In doing so, we too benefit in untold, unimaginable ways. The universe has a magnificent habit of rewarding souls for such bravery, boldness and greatness. As ever, the choice is yours.

In any attempt to expand your horizons, you are bound to encounter challenges and obstacles. It is essential you are tested, tests demonstrate our conviction and these challenges are a fundamental aspect of growth. We have to battle for that sweet victory. Watch any Olympic sport and observe the sheer joy in the faces of winners crossing the finishing line. They are ecstatic. You cannot fake that feeling and it moves me every single time. Those winning Olympians are in a heightened state where all the blood, sweat, pain and tears are crystallised into a euphoric moment of utter jubilation. At any given point, in the years of dedication to their craft, they could have given up, quit, thrown in the towel, called it a day, partied with friends and turned their back on their dreams. But something compelled them - to push through and fight on. Failure was always an option, but not one they were willing to indulge. What I believe we witness as they cross that finishing line is their personal miracle, their special moment in time, where dedication and sacrifice come together in a momentous victory. It's no wonder they can barely contain themselves. Hats off to those athletes: they grafted for that gold, sacrificed for that gold, dedicated themselves for that gold. What do you need to dedicate yourself to, to get your personal gold? What do you need to sacrifice? What do you need to surrender? Most people, whether athletes or not, are not prepared to make the sacrifices necessary to get what they really want. They sacrifice the gold for valueless meandering that does little for themselves, let alone anyone else. You have the potential. It's innate and in every single one of us. The choice, however is always yours and Netflix always has a shiny new box set series for you to binge upon.

If you believe that change will be plain sailing or if you recoil at the first hurdle then, sorry to say, it is highly unlikely you are ready. Change takes resilience, hope, grit, fear, faith, perseverance, determination, focus, and sacrifice. If I am brutally honest, most folks turn and walk away when the obstacles arise. They see challenge as an insurmountable mountain. They see challenge as an indicator that they should not try. They see challenge as a sign that they are punching above their weight. Challenge-averse folks see obstacles as a sign that they need to get back in their box, that they were naïve to dream. Sadly, this often results in their turning on their heels and walking away. It's at this point that valuable life lessons are missed. Expect to be challenged! There really needs to be education around this topic, to help us understand the process. Too many people abandon ship. Making a decision to change our life is fantastic, but it is just the beginning: there is no straight road to glory. When we don't understand this fact we are significantly disadvantaged, and the likelihood of our transition is hampered. **The obstacle is the way.**

When we choose to give up up on our dreams, we turn our back on our potential. We settle for a life of mediocrity, playing small, with diminished personal power. At worst, this can feed and fuel depression. I have witnessed it time and time again in my therapeutic work, where my clients reveal their unmet dreams. I often hear problem-focused statements, elaborate justifications and excuses as to why they didn't believe it could be done. Ultimately, they have settled for less and, at some gut level, feel uncomfortable about their choices. But fret not: you may have turned your back on your dream, but your dream will never turn its back on you. The urge may subside, you may even ignore it altogether, but like that splinter still lurking deep in your big right toe, it will prod and poke you, at unexpected times, just to remind you gently that it's going nowhere!

BLOCKS TO SELF-LOVE: INFORMATION OVERLOAD

Knowledge is power! Well, I beg to disagree. We live in the information age now, and we have access to vast amounts of information in a matter of moments. No more reaching for the Encyclopaedia Britannica or heading off to the British Library. So much can be found at the end of our fingertips, with our so-called smart devices. We are in the age of information overload and a battle rages for our attention. Social media platforms want us to stay on for longer, and the rising tide of clickbait is upon us. We can google, watch videos, download books, listen to podcasts, subscribe to newsletters and pay for membership sites. Data is the new crude oil and it all starts with handing over our email address. We are more distracted than ever: just look at people walking down the street, glued to their phones. We are slowly becoming obsessed with likes, comments, stats and shares. Combined with the fact that 'social' media giants change algorithms to manipulate, control and predict our behaviour (not to mention win elections), we really have little idea of the damaging impact our smart devices are having on our humanity.

In my view, knowledge in itself is no longer power. We no longer have any excuse not to be in the know - it is how we apply knowledge that holds the true power. This may be the greatest challenge for our generation. I recall a rainy afternoon in June. I had forgotten my umbrella, and my daughter looked baffled and asked: 'Don't you check the forecast on your phone before you leave?' 'No' I replied. She looked perplexed. As this was standard practice for her, she couldn't comprehend why it was not the same for me. That situation got me thinking: yes, the weather forecast is one click away, but this information is not a priority for me, as it is for her. A valuable lesson came from this innocent encounter. We prioritise what's personally important to us and disregard the rest. Humans have limited attention capacity for very good reasons. So, when it comes to the matter of being our greatest self, the truth is, if we really want it, then we need to make it a priority in our lives. There are distractions aplenty, now more than ever, and we need to become disciplined, focused and keep our eye on the prize.

Take for example, the modern phenomenon that is Netflix. This media mogul has an ever-increasing library of box sets, films and documentaries to keep you entertained. 'Boxset-binge' has become a part of everyday language and, at times, I have wondered whether it is a contributory factor that feeds the growing tide of anxiety and depression in the Western world. It does not strike me as a healthy practice to go from duvet day to duvet day while consuming hours upon hours of 'Orange Is the New Black'. Forgive me, but would it not be better for your mental and physical health, to get up, get out, and take in your surroundings? Heaven forbid, you could even try a short media studies course if you love TV that much. Channel your passion or channel-surf. The choice is always yours.

I am not here to judge. I am here to poke and prod those that have a curious mind. Mass consumption of media was not as drastic a challenge ten years ago. Now, more than ever, we need to be acutely aware of mindless distractions and to develop disciplined action in order to move up and beyond our comfort zone. This will not be easy: we are becoming addicted. If we really want to break entrenched limiting patterns that keep us playing small, keep us broke and in vicious cycles, then we need to get serious and prioritise our actions. The reality is that there are many more vices, temptations and distractions to navigate in current times.

We have untold potential within us, waiting to be unearthed, and we must be disciplined if we want to extricate that gold. Otherwise we won't make it, and our deepest ambitions will be pipe dreams. We are the creators of our reality and the authors of our lives, so if we do not learn to shut out the noise, we will fall foul of the powerful media moguls' persuasive, seductive, distracting force.

BLOCKS TO SELF-LOVE: INTERNAL HURDLES

Internal barriers to self-love are real and relentless. The thinking skills that propelled your growth in 2008 may well be redundant in 2018. If you have a dominant negative voice in your head, your personal Cruella de Vil, then know that she is a slippery sucker, a chameleon, that evolves and grows with you. So beware: she will catch you off-guard and is always waiting in the wings to sabotage your dreams. I cannot state enough how important it is to develop a relationship with your inner critic. She holds incredible power over your life. She is the voice that feeds panic attacks, depression and anxiety. She can make you believe you are not good-enough and, if you happen to be a perfectionist, she governs your life. Nothing ever meets the mark and, if you're not careful, she can make it an utter misery. Believe it or not, she often has good intentions, and that's why you need to get to befriend her. Building a relationship with this unruly aspect of yourself is fundamental to self-love, and to your desire to become your greatest self.

Encountering obstacles is a given rite of passage, if we truly desire to change and become a better version of ourselves. Obstacles are there to test us; to build our muscle and conviction; to aid us on our journey. **Forewarned is forearmed**. Being able to differentiate the types of obstacles is particularly helpful. Are they internal obstacles, something to do with the limitations of our thinking or skills? Or are they factors in the external world that are hindering our growth? Knowing the difference is the key to helping us find the right solutions for our pinch points. Embrace the ride.

We only have one life to live, so let's live it. None of us is promised tomorrow.

The internal blocks that we encounter as we learn to love ourselves can be vast. As previously said, one of the biggest threats is Cruella de Vil and her negative self-talk. She is an incredibly harsh inner critic who chastises, mocks and instils dread and fear as we attempt to change. We need to pay close attention to her. **Our inner dialogue holds the key to our growth**, as our self-talk influences our thoughts, beliefs and most importantly our behaviour. If our Cruella de Vil (or whatever we like to call that part of us) is particularly harsh and brutal, and takes up most of our thinking, it may benefit us to get some professional help, which will assist us in becoming familiar with our inner critic. Often, this voice wants us to stay in the stagnation of the comfort zone, where it perceives that we feel safe, and there will be minimal exposure to shame and humiliation. Cruella de Vil may mean well, but we need to understand her motives, openly acknowledge her voice, see how she works and what fear is fuelling her fire. In doing so, we are taking brave and bold steps to self-knowledge and, potentially, self-mastery.

Examples of internal blocks:
- Addiction
- Lack of self-care
- Poor diet
- Limiting beliefs
- Lack of sleep
- Lack of exercise
- Unresolved past hurts / traumas
- Pessimistic mindset
- Instant gratification
- Procrastination
- Physical disabilities
- Perfectionism

- Unhelpful self-talk
- Lack of patience
- Too many ideas
- Starting but not completing tasks
- Stubbornness
- Self-hatred
- Fear of the unknown
- Fear of success
- Disorganisation
- Distraction
- Self-sabotage
- Comparison
- Guilt and shame
- Avoidance
- Self-chastisement

BLOCKS TO SELF-LOVE: EXTERNAL BARRIERS

External barriers to self-love are as real and relentless as internal barriers. Some psychologists convincingly argue that the external environment is not as important as our inner world; that it is the way that we personally think, believe, and respond to external events that sets the tone for the quality of our lives. But while there is much merit in this viewpoint, I would be negligent if I did not honour the complexities of the external environment, too. It is beneficial to explore and assess our external world through a critical lens, so as to help us to understand how our environment permits or inhibits our ability to practise self-love. A personal self-love SWOT test (strengths, weaknesses, opportunities, threats) will assist us in getting a practical overview of the factors that we may need to consider when deciding to make changes to our lives.

Patricia is a high-profile managing director with three children and a partner diagnosed with multiple sclerosis. There is no physical or sexual aspect to their relationship and, over time, she has reluctantly become her partner's carer, which she is increasingly resenting. In addition, her partner is bitter about his situation and tends to take his frustrations out on the family. Over the years his mood has got worse, and Patricia has taken to spending more time at work to avoid the tension and stress in the family home.

Patricia hasn't had a holiday in a long time and, although she would like to get away, the guilt keeps her stuck. Slowly her resentment builds and her well-being declines. Patricia misses intimacy and longs for wild, passionate sex. She mutes her desires, but recently found herself flirting at an office party. What began fairly innocently bubbled over into a full-blown, rip-your-knickers-off, passion-filled affair. Six months later, the affair crashes and burns and Patricia is dumped. She is devastated. By the time her employer refers her to Key for Change for therapy, she has been off work for three months suffering from depression.

Patricia is broken, but the catalyst issue (the affair) is not the root cause. To get to the heart of the matter, we have needed to explore more deeply, to unearth the many small ways in which she has dishonoured herself. As a therapist, my ambition is to assist her to understand why she puts herself last, and to discover where and why this behaviour began. Additionally, I want to understand what benefits being selfless hold for her. This is especially important since, when we change any type of behaviour, there will be loss. It's important that I get a sense of what that loss will be, because if it is not exposed there will be an underlying resistance that may hinder the therapeutic process.

For example, Patricia was asked by friends to go away for the weekend to celebrate a 40th birthday. She instantly declined, saying that it would be selfish, and that she wouldn't be able to handle the feelings of guilt if she left her husband. Work was always an acceptable reason to leave the house. Anything other than that, she considered to be self-indulgent and a sign that she did not care about her family. Insight into this dynamic helped me to understand the full extent of Patricia's selfless identity. Her entire character was built around putting everyone else first. Therefore, any action that challenged this dynamic was perceived as a massive threat, and as such was met with sheer stubborn resistance. This was a golden insight. It helped me to understand Patricia at a deeper level and sparked my curiosity about how guilt, shame and selfishness functioned in her life. It also left me ever more curious about what life experiences, or people, had inspired her thinking.

As therapy proceeds, it will further expose Patricia's internal blocks (her thinking world) and the external ones (family demands, work commitments) that hinder her from being true to herself. We will explore her past, to identify the root cause of her thinking and the purpose that fuels her selfless giving. Her psychological world is being unknitted, and the delicate process of becoming self-aware is under way. As previously observed, new behaviour is a massive threat to her identity, so small, self-selected changes are often the best place to begin. As time goes by, and Patricia's awareness heightens, hopefully she will get to the point where she can make conscious choices as to whether she acts in self-nurturing or self-deprecating ways. As ever, the choice is hers.

Patricia's scenario is a brief example of how applying self-love to one's life can be complex, because of external factors that need to be considered. Balancing these competing variables is not easy. At times, it can feel that there will be too many repercussions if we change. It is often fear that keeps us stuck, trying to make untenable situations work. Over time, it is likely that denial, distortion and avoidance will become the norm for Patricia as she continuously tries to ignore her own needs. But the human spirit is fierce and will find all manner of coercive ways to get its needs met. What we deny, distort or avoid has a way of coming back with a vengeance, and when it does there will be problems. When we do not confront tricky situations, we are setting ourselves up for bigger problems later. Bigger problems are even trickier to resolve. We can deal with the problems now, while they are still manageable, or later, when they have got out of hand. The choice is ours.

Examples of external demands:

- Society's demands

49

- Jobs / work commitments
- Boss
- Family
- Commitments
- Responsibilities
- Finances
- Class
- Culture / religion
- Other people's opinions
- Access to opportunities
- Access to networks
- Support (or lack of it)
- Family honour / reputation / expectations
- Location
- WiFi access

SELF-LOVE AUDIT: THE PHONE

Our phones. We love them, we hate them; we can't be without them. We charge them, they die; we forget them, we turn back; we lose them, we find them; we break them, we fix them. We feel naked without them. How has it come to this? They have passwords, codes and fingerprint recognition. We don't want anyone getting in. We store appointments, emails, photos, bank accounts, bank statements, contacts, and favourite videos. We get access to the world via the web. We know we spend way too much time on our phones but, like Pringles, they are hard to resist. Most, if not all, of our lives can be found in various nooks and crannies on our devices – so, in considering our main topic, it is important to be aware that our phones offer untold opportunities for practising (or for not practising) self-love.

Social media has us continuously connected, but there is a downside to continuous connectedness, especially when relationships go sour. It is increasingly recognised that social media complicates the break-up process. For example, what if we are constantly tempted to search for our ex-partner online? It can, let's face it, be hard to fight that feeling and at certain weak moments we may succumb. With so much **continuous connection** it's no wonder that curiosity gets the better of us. What if we are secretly stalking our ex-partner online? We need to ask ourselves: is this really good for us? Or does it keep us holding on, and prolong the healing process?

Take for example the simple matter of a WhatsApp profile picture change by your ex. He displays a picture of himself hugging an attractive woman, and this has you in a frenzy. You ruminate on the 1001 potential covert messages he is trying to send. You're furious and go on mission payback, where you desperately seek to up the ante. But it's all fake; you are hurt and the pain is eating you up inside. This can send you into a desperate tail spin and, simply put, is not good for you. In essence, you're doing yourself a great disservice. Behind all the fake smiles, at nights you cannot sleep, you can't get your ex out of your mind and you really are not helping yourself to move on. You need to consider seriously whether remaining 'connected' is in your best interests. You must ask: am I acting in self-loving ways? Such a question goes straight to the heart of the matter, and may evoke stubborn resistance. The truth is that, often, we don't really want to let go and I do get it. Its not easy to go against yourself, but there comes a time when we need to put coping strategies in place. This is one of the reasons why I created the WhatsApp sanity tool that gives you 15 self-care tips to help you look after you (**you can find this tool at the Key for Change website, under the resources section**).

If we choose to use them, there are more and more features on our phones that have the potential to protect us from self-sabotage. For example, the block feature. I am a big fan. At times, it may be in our best interests to block, unfriend or unfollow people, if we are taking active steps to move on. Just consider: you love someone, you desperately want them in your life, and they are playing mind games. Then your phone becomes an incredible source of anxiety and stress, and can feed into depression. Taking medication may well have its place, but if you fail to cleanse your device, you are setting yourself up for problems. Believe it or not, you do have a choice, you do not have to be a sitting duck. There are self-loving measures that you can put in place, if you are prepared to face your fears, be kind to yourself, and let go with dignity, style and grace.

Yes, it can be done. There will be times when it is an act of self-love to remove yourself from certain social media platforms, and to remove certain apps. At times, it can be an act of self-love to turn the damn phone off, or to leave it at home or even in the car for an hour. Give yourself some respite. Heaven forbid, you could consider getting a new number, do an entire clean-out. This is particularly important if you are battling with self-loathing and tend to compare yourself to others. Or are you someone who is waiting for the two blue WhatsApp ticks when you message someone significant? If so, this can be painful, especially when you see that they're online and you're being ignored. My encouragement to you, is to pay close attention to whether your phone makes you feel better, or if it fills you with anxiety and dread. If the latter is the case, then it may be important that you 'sanitise' it, delete contacts, remove triggering pictures, even take the drastic action of changing your number. Do something, anything, that you deem necessary to promote self-loving ways. Remember, you will not always like the decisions you have to make in order to love and nurture yourself. It's all about self-protection and self-preservation here. At times, you will have to **defy yourself to be kind to yourself.** Let's be honest, it is your responsibility to look after yourself, and your phone is a powerful vehicle for acts of self-love or self-harm. Only you can decide.

SELF-LOVE AUDIT: WHAT WE BRING TO RELATIONSHIPS

The foundations for love should be established by our parents and caregivers in our early years (generally 0-7). According to Maslow's hierarchy of needs theory, we will fail to self-actualise if our basic needs are not met. One of those essential needs is love. If we do not receive safe, consistent love at that formative stage, then the consequences can be disastrous for our self-worth in adult life. We will notice this void most acutely in our intimate relationships, where we seek mutual love, compatibility, comfort and companionship. Ultimately, the way in which we were loved by our parents sets the tone for future relationships. If we could not trust our parents, it's likely that we will replicate this experience with our partners. Unconsciously, we seek out relationships that repeat familiar pain. It's annoyingly true. So, if you are baffled by the lack of safe, consistent love in your intimate relationships, or you have noticed that you tend to repeat unhelpful patterns, then the answer may lie in exploring the way that you yourself were loved in your younger years.

Looking into our past is particularly helpful if we want to understand the relationship problems that we are experiencing today. As a psychotherapist, I am acutely aware that looking back and going deeper into the past can be difficult - especially if we have bad memories that we do not want to recall. But **remember, the truth will always set us free.** What is in the dark we cannot see, and what we cannot see wreaks havoc at an unconscious level. The result of our blindness sneaks through, often without our permission, into unhelpful behaviour that ends up causing us problems. The obstacle is the way, and I am a firm believer that at times we need to go back in order to understand the root causes of issues today. Now, if that speaks to you, then my encouragement will always be that you seek professional help.

Here are a few questions that I ask my clients to kickstart their thinking:

What benefits do you gain from being in this relationship?

What is it about you that enables people to take advantage of you?

What justifications have you given to others that allow them to ill-treat you?

The truth of it all, is that we teach people how to treat us. So, if you find that you are perpetually in unhelpful, abusive, toxic or unfulfilling relationships, then it may benefit you to stop looking outwards and take a deep dive within.

SELF-LOVE AUDIT: YOUR CAREER

You may have felt a calling to a particular profession, or have held a secret desire to pursue a totally new career. Or perhaps you have had a dream that is so big it frightens you, and for years you have ignored the recurring signs that it is sending you. Then, like me, you will know that this burning desire for something different, something bigger, never leaves you. The feeling may subside, but the flame flickers on, nudging, poking and reminding you that something different is waiting for you.

Work takes up most of our lives and, if you are in a job you hate, then this will be an area where a lack of self-love impacts on the quality of your life. You may have had wide-eyed dreams of becoming a pilot, author, psychologist, doctor, musician, historian or International DJ, but for whatever reason the dream became elusive, family members disapproved, or life got busy and your dreams got sidelined. I am fascinated by people's abandoned ambitions, hobbies and dreams. I do believe that, wrapped up in some of these sidelined pursuits, there can hide a hidden gem that is intrinsically connected to our purpose. It may sound rather fanciful and fluffy. However, I believe that if we pursue these interests with commitment and intention, we may begin to move towards Maslow's 'self-actualisation', the realisation or fulfilment of our potential.

If we feel fulfilled at work, yet rubbish in all other areas of our life, then this is also a matter of concern. Dynamics at work can change in a heartbeat for several internal and external reasons. For example, we may have a new power-hungry boss, or the loss of a contract may result in redundancy. A new government may come into power and, as a result, our service goes through radical change and we are forced to re-apply for our current role (the ultimate insult). If most of our identity is attached to a role or job title, then we will be incredibly vulnerable when changes occur at work. **Remember: nothing ever stays the same.** So, it is beneficial that we are proactive in protecting ourselves against this inevitability.

One way to counteract the inevitability of workplace changes, is to discover what we truly love and to take small consistent steps to bring more of it into our lives. This is an act of self-love, as we are giving ourselves permission to honour our needs. There may well be another unexpected bonus, where we accidentally stumble across our calling. You see, the sad reality is that most people never take the time to sit down and think about what it is that they really want for themselves. I believe we're here on planet earth to do something wonderful with our lives. Our ultimate challenge is to find out what that wonderful thing is, and then to pour our energy into pursuing it. That passion is what gives our lives purpose and meaning, plus enables us to grow into better versions of ourselves.

My questions to you are: what lights your fire? what is your heart's desire? These are important life questions, and they throw up even more questions about the possible reasons for the rapid rise of depression in the western world - such as whether it relates to a lack of purpose and meaning in people's lives rather than deficit brains in need of more and more medication. That is not something that we will be able to explore in this book, but I do know from personal experience that, when we discover and pursue our calling, our lives take new directions, into uncharted and unimagined territory. Such exploration can be deeply fulfilling, as we open ourselves up to new experiences. We have all heard the quote: **find a job you love and you will never work again.** My personal story colours my view here, but having the courage to pursue my dreams has changed my life beyond all recognition. Life has a way of rewarding you when you are bold enough to believe in yourself. I am empowered, feel more in control, and take full responsibility for my life. Simultaneously, I also respect why people sometimes do not make the sacrifices required to honour their dreams. **Remember, the road to self-actualisation is not a smooth one.** Many people will have the desire and potential, but not the will or the courage to push through the various obstacles and diversions that will inevitably crop up along the way. Interestingly, I can understand the reasons why people let go of their dreams. The terrain is indeed rugged, and the struggle is real. As ever, **I respect free will.**

When it comes to our careers, we are often the first to stifle and squash our own dreams. We play small, we stay in comfort zones that get filled with dread and fear, we find 101 reasons not to make a change. Elaborate excuses. Comfortable stories. Ultimately, we are selling ourselves short and we know it. When we continuously say no to ourselves, or wait for our boss to accord us approval, we are not acting in our best interests. When we refuse to give ourselves permission to pursue our passions, we are operating in fear: fear of the unknown, fear of our potential, fear of leaving the comfort zone or, even more baffling, fear of success. Far too often, it is this type of fear that keeps people stuck - stuck in a rut, stuck in jobs they hate, stuck with a desire to try something different, yet somehow paralysed. And so another year passes by, and the next thing it's been ten years in a lacklustre job. Slowly, it becomes the norm. We talk the talk, but we don't walk the walk. At worst, we become a moaner. We complain about the problem but take no action to resolve it. Before we know it, it's been fifteen years and we're gridlocked. To add insult to injury, we may be sacked or made redundant, expected to do more and more for less and less, or made so ill by the job that we go off sick.

When we bring self-love into our careers, we take radical self-responsibility for our dreams and ambitions. We do not wait for others to give us opportunities. We create them. We invest in ourselves and give ourselves permission to pursue our passion. **So my questions to you are:**

What has stopped you from fulfilling your potential?

Why do you stay so long in a job that you hate?

What is the one small act you can do today to regain control over your career?

Ultimately, one of the biggest blocks to unlocking our career potential is our reluctance to give ourselves permission and come face to face with our fears. When we continuously look to others to give us the head nod, when we do not look within ourselves to validate our choices, we lose our personal power. Such a loss cannot be underestimated. A loss of personal power is directly linked to depression, and if we live a disempowered life then it is only natural that our spirit will wane. The famous Italian sculptor Michelangelo chipped away at disregarded marble to reveal his masterpiece. Your greatest masterpiece lives inside you, and you need to chip away at the parts that camouflage your greatness. Hidden within you is a gem that has been waiting to be discovered the whole time. It is your duty to reveal it, piece by piece, stone by stone. Depression is a sign, people, a sign that there is a discord, a misalignment; a sign that you are out of sync with your authentic selves, a sign that there is disharmony. The question is: when will you start to chip away at the parts of you that no longer serve you? As ever, only you can decide.

WORKING ON THE SELF

When we start to work on ourselves, we are in a small yet profound way beginning the process of saying yes to ourselves. It is the beginning of a personal revolution. While this may not seem epic, the reality is that far too often our lives are built upon our saying yes to everyone but ourselves. We don't know when it happened or how we got to this position, it's been a slow subtle creeper, but somehow we have ended up neglecting ourselves. When being selfless is the norm, we gradually become disconnected from our authentic self. As time goes by, we find ourselves increasingly out of sync with it. Furthermore, we also underplay or ignore our successes and triumphs and exaggerate our failings. It's no wonder that we end up depressed: we really are not nice to ourselves.

When you begin to say yes to yourself, you disrupt well-worn patterns, and people will not always welcome the change. When folk reject, ridicule or question the new you, this backlash will hurt, especially when the criticism comes from your family. Ironically, it might have been family members who told you in the first place that you needed to 'fix up'. Now that you have finally dusted yourself down, pushed through your fears, and taken bold steps, it is those closest to you who may turn out to be your biggest adversaries. The mixed messages are incredibly confusing and enough to drive you berserk. Fret not: expect this type of turbulence on the self-love journey. **The obstacle is the way.** You are being tested.

When you actively start to change, you are upsetting people's perceptions of you. Humans love short cuts, and getting to know the new you will take time and patience as you shed your old skin and grow into a new version. As such, you will challenge their previous expectations of you. Some will hate your change; others will encourage you. Your duty is to know who is safe, and to limit your time with energy vampires. People may indirectly tell you to get back in your box, or be so bold as to ask, 'who do you think you are?' Worse still, they may remind you to 'know your place'. Utter nonsense! The truth is, people around you will be uncomfortable with change, so it will be natural for them to resist. They are not used to the new, emerging you and you are getting used to the change yourself, so expect external resistance and find ways to fortify yourself during the transition. And note that you must fortify yourself especially against resistance from your family. They are the people whose opinion, we often care about, but they will be the most wedded to old ideas of you, and at times will be made anxious and fearful by your change.

A word of caution: pay close attention to guilt trippers. They'll use subtle or covert manipulative tactics to get you to fall into line, and this is often one of the biggest threats to change. You will have to look for a message in the mayhem, and build a trusted support network that nurtures and encourages you. Change is not easy, but neither is being stuck. When you stay stuck, you go round in dizzying circles. **Remember, nothing good in life comes easy**.

THE KEY: HOW CHANGE HAPPENS

Self-awareness is a journey, and one that I hope will last you a lifetime. There will be twists and turns, ups and downs. That is a given. Expect it. There is a rhythm to life, if we can catch the beat. How we react and respond is always key, and hidden within our choices is an infinite power that has the potential to revolutionise our lives. As a psychotherapist, I am in the business of helping people to become their greatest self. One aspect of what I do is to help them become increasingly self-aware. The more aware we become, the more we can make empowered choices. There are times when we are WOKE and we still 'sell ourselves short'. If this is the case, then it's likely that an inferiority complex is wreaking havoc and that we are battling with feelings of unworthiness or not being good enough. Either way, trust the process. Nothing good comes quickly and we are developing long-lasting change here, so we have to be patient with ourselves, even when we are selling ourselves short. Self-awareness is the key. It takes us out of the dark of unconscious reaction and into the light of consciousness. Life is the playground where we get to learn, play and practise. We must not fret if we screw up. As long as we are breathing, we can always try again. Life gifts us with an abundance of opportunities, and important life lessons can be hidden in the most adverse of experiences.

Before my training as a therapist, I often found myself in relationships with people who were 'takers'. They always needed something, and I was only too pleased to give. I thought that this was standard protocol for a loving relationship - after all, it was what I witnessed growing up. Giving made me feel good, and served a need in me. I became a perpetual rescuer and, in the end, I gave too much and put myself in a precarious position. My wake-up call came when I fell in love with a narcissist. In this whirlwind, all-consuming romance my giving, selfless ways expanded to their fullest extent and, as a well-established 'fixer', I soon made his problems my own. I would swoop in and find a multitude of solutions for the multitude of problems he created. Nothing was ever too much trouble. In the end, I got into financial hardship, almost lost my job, got bad credit, and had to flee the family home for the safety of a women's refuge. I compromised my firm footing to help someone I loved, and got sucked in, dragged down, and almost taken under.

Loving a narcissistic man is far from easy, and today I believe that it was a situation I unconsciously co-created. It was also one that has been instrumental in my growth and change. Yes: I was young, naïve and desperate for love, but when the warning lights flashed at me, I put my foot on the throttle in a bid to prove how loyal and committed I could be. In the words of Meatloaf, I would do anything for love. The reality is that when we choose to ignore all the warning signs, red flags, disrespect, disloyalty and betrayal - when we turn a blind eye, sweep problems under the rug or, worse, pretend that the problems don't exist and opt for what some describe as ignorant bliss - we are setting ourselves up for a major catastrophe in the future. As such, today I understand that I was complicit in my abuse. People often resist this truth, they kick against it, get really angry and lash out against it. But it's my truth and I wholeheartedly acknowledge it.

In the main, it seems that we like some aspects of self-responsi-bility - just not all of it. But the truth will always set you free. I embrace self-responsibility. It can be a bitter pill to swallow but, like cough medicine, it will do you good. Today, at this precise moment, I find it rather freeing to know that if I create my reality, through the vehicle of my choices, then - in any given situation - I am free to make new choices, to shift my gaze to new horizons. Earlier on, I was not self-aware, and my critical eye was firmly shut. I did the best that I could, based on my knowledge at that particular time. So, I do not beat myself up, nor do I have any regrets. I am kind to myself. Back then I was in the dark (unconscious) and, from that difficult catastrophic situation, I have stepped into the light (self-aware). Today, I am in the privileged position of proclaiming that I am grateful for what I went through.

The cold harsh reality is that a life without personal boundaries is not a pretty one. Back in 2001, I was lost, confused, and did not understand how I had gotten myself into such a dire situation. I blamed him, took no responsibility, and felt like a victim. I was always rescuing him from the calamity and chaos he created. I set myself up as Superwoman. He felt utterly confident and reassured that I would find a solution to his issues, and he was right. I always did. But then, I got pregnant, life got routine, structured and serious. He got bored and found someone else exciting, unattached and childless, so my time was up and I was on the back bench. Years of rescuing took its toll. I was drained of energy and, by the end, I was the one left broken. When my back was against the wall, he was nowhere to be seen. He was done with me. I was washed up, used up, and he was off to 'better things'. That's one of the most interesting aspects of being a perpetual giver: you think you're irreplaceable, you think that a person can't function without you, that they need you. The reality is that you are a tool, a person of convenience and a disposable commodity.

Inspired by my wake-up call, I started to read self-help books. I soon came to realise that I was totally in the dark, never acknowledged my needs, and was continuously 'other-focused'. Today, I believe that selfless giving can only be sustained for a finite amount of time. Why? Because it is so utterly draining and exhausting. It's a one-way relationship. Plus, when your own needs crop up and you want the other person to return the favour, they often flee the scene. They have had their fill and did not sign up for mutual exchange. There is no reciprocity. In the end, you compromise yourself. It's an inevitable consequence. Developing self-awareness is a process. The veil may slowly be removed from your eyes, or your situation may catapult you quite suddenly into getting WOKE. Either way, when you become increasingly self-aware and begin to develop an inner relationship with yourself, the rose-tinted spectacles come off and your insights can start to become truly profound.

PROGRESSING TOWARDS SELF-AWARENESS

Today, as a therapist, my ambition is to assist my clients to develop self-insight, self-responsibility and awareness of the consequences of their choices. This process, of coming out of the dark (unaware of self) and into the light, appears to go through certain stages that I have observed both in myself and in the lives of others. I hope that my articulation is of help. It is a work in progress.

(a) Blind/unaware of self We are unaware, clueless - and things are happening to us. We do not understand how they happen or how we engineer these situations. In fact, we do not even understand that we are also orchestrating the process. Often, we feel like a victim. How could they do this to me? Why me? 'Poor me' thinking is prevalent. If we were in a boat, we would have no oars and the tide would be taking us wherever it went. We feel as though we have no control.

(b) The pinch Something about our behaviour or an external situation starts to cause us problems. When we get a pinch, our curiosity is aroused. We inspect the wound and give it a rub. The emotional pain makes its mark, but not enough to prompt any meaningful action. So we brush it off - push the issue to one side, or sweep it under the rug. Avoidance. We may carry on regardless, but the pinch has left an uncomfortable sting.

(c) The wallop The pinch turns into a full wallop. The pain is

undeniable, we are bamboozled, disoriented, and catapulted into a harsh uncomfortable reality - a reality that we have been avoiding. The wallop is incredibly shocking, and we may not even have seen it coming. This profound blow has brought us to our knees, knocked us off our feet, and we're not sure whether we can get up again. We may even question whether life is worth living. The time for denial is over. We have had a major blow and we're wounded. We need healing. Our wound needs inspecting. We can't go on in the same way. Our coping strategies are redundant. Nothing is working. It's time to face the music. This may well be a rock-bottom experience for us and, if it is, we should welcome it: it has the potential to revolutionise our lives.

It is in this dark, difficult, hurtful place, when the chips are down, the odds are stacked against us, and our backs are firmly against the wall, that there can be no more denial. We inspect our wounds. The cut is deep, it's colossal. It's a gaping injury that requires immediate attention. We need to understand and learn more about what has happened to us. At this time, we experience confusion, sleepless nights, increased inner conflict, sadness, despair, bewilderment, utter agony. We can't concentrate and our whole world is turned upside down. People are worried for us. We're not ourselves. We may have gone to the doctor and may be off work sick. There's no question that the situation needs some immediate attention. The pain is crippling and at times it feels as if we will never move beyond it. It is usually at this point that people call me.

(d) Awakening The process of gaining awareness is in its sapling phase. Our eyes are slowly opening and we begin to see life though a new lens. We start to notice and grow in our understanding of external dynamics that hinder and harm us. If we are open and non-defensive, we will be able to embrace the idea that we are responsible for our actions. We begin to see the small ways in which

we have sold ourselves short, how we mute our truth or how easy it is to fall back into old entrenched patterns. If we are in therapy, we may experiment with new behaviours and feel excited by the new reactions we encounter. We may begin to play with the idea that we create our reality. If we are resistant during this phase, or do not want to face up fully to the severity of our situation, or want to circumnavigate responsibility, we will still seek out people and situations on which we can lay blame. In this phase, our defences become exposed. It can be a painful process. If you are working with me, then understand that I am the Dettol that cleans the wound. I do this using inconvenient truths, truths that can hurt and sting but that, in the long run, will free you and heal you. In the awakening phase, if you allow me, and decide truly to invest in yourself, I will hold up a mirror to you. If you are willing and open - open even in your resistance - you will start to see a new dawn arising.

(e) New visions You may well still be selling yourself short. But now you know exactly what you are doing. In this phase, although you feel powerless to change your behaviour, you are catching yourself in the act of self-sabotage. This is particularly important, because the more you can do this, the more empowered you will become to make different choices. Self-awareness is one of the most important aspects of the change process. At times, you may slip into old unhelpful patterns, and it pisses you off that you are backsliding again. You annoy yourself: why can't I just apply the knowledge? Be encouraged. You are now in the privileged position of being able to catch yourself with your 'hand in the cookie jar'; and remember - there was a time when you were totally unaware. So fret not: this type of insight is key to change.

Let's take that cookie analogy one step further, as time goes by, you will, I hope, go from finding your hand already in the cookie jar to watching your hand in the act of reaching out for the sweet treats. Catching yourself earlier and earlier is the key. When you catch yourself, you can stop and ask yourself a few important questions, such as: 'Do I really want to do this?' 'What do I need to do to regain control?' 'Why am I doing this?' 'What is my intuition telling me?' This type of detailed self-enquiry is fundamental to change and enables you to uncover the deeper motives behind your behaviour. You go from being filled with regret about eating your tenth cookie, to catching your right hand flinching. It's when your hand flinches that you start to get curious and ask those important questions.

This cookie analogy works for whatever challenge you're experiencing. Say you keep on ending up in bed with 'Won't commit Fred'. Did you realise that, by sending the innocent 'hey you' text, you took one step closer to being in Fred's company? Often, your actions are making it happen and, if Fred makes you unhappy, then when you initiate contact with him, sorry to say, you're inviting misery into your life. At some unconscious level, you want to sleep with him. Your biggest challenge is that you are in denial and not being real with yourself about your underlying motives. Lying to yourself is exhausting: it takes a lot of work to override your inner wisdom and truth. Therefore, you're likely to go on a mission to convince yourself that it was an innocent text but, really, your text was loaded. You know it. In fact, you wanted to meet him, and you just don't want to admit it to yourself.

It may not feel great, because you said that the last time would be the last. Again, you may be baffled that despite all your self-awareness you are still screwing yourself over. But take heart: you are learning all the time, and getting access to the various intricate ways in which you are sabotaging yourself. These insights are priceless. The key here is how much you are prepared to be brutally truthful with yourself. If you are not willing to admit your shortcomings, or if you are stubborn and defensive, then this phase will be hard and you will want to abandon ship altogether. But don't lose heart, you're nearly there.

CHOICE: THE REVELATION - BEING WOKE

Now that your self-awareness is getting stronger, it's as if you can observe yourself from a detached viewpoint. You have the privilege of catching yourself just before you undertake self-sabotaging behaviours. For example, you are moving from 'ending up in bed with Fred', to catching yourself sending the catalyst 'hey you' text. You should now come to realise that you are co-creating the situation, creating your misery, because of the choices you make. Simple as that!

When you are fully woke, you have the option to stop yourself by not reacting in your old familiar patterns. So, when you feel an urge to reach for your phone and scroll to find Fred's number, you are aware of exactly what you are doing. You are instigating the contact and you know it. It did not just happen! You engineered your misery though your choices. So hit the send button or call him. It's totally up to you. Now that you are so beautifully self-aware, you pause before you give in to your urge to text him (stimulus gap). You pay close attention to your thoughts and feelings. You get curious about what triggered you. Always try to follow the 'what triggered me' thread, trace backwards, see what you find. I tell you, there is gold in such discoveries, if you can learn to trust the process. When you trace backwards, you may find a deeper, more profound reason for reaching out. For instance, 'If I stopped seeing him, then there would be no male interest.' 'No one would want me, I would be totally alone.' 'I hate being alone, it's excruciating. I would rather have something than nothing at all.'

Once you have given yourself some space to consider your triggers and deeper fears, you can decide mindfully what to do, being more aware and more real with yourself. Old behaviour or new? The choice is always yours. This is a process where you go from impulsive reaction - 'let me send him a text' - to responding in a well-considered, thought-through manner. In this instance, you are not simply reacting. You are responding from a place where you are mindful not only of your choices, but of the consequences of your decisions. Additionally, you are being real with yourself: if you send this 'hey you' text, you are taking one step closer to seeing him tonight. You are then free to ask yourself, 'Do I just want sex? Or is it closeness and intimacy?' 'What is my deeper motive here? What am I avoiding?' 'What do I really get from this relationship? What need does this relationship feed in me?' At some level, a need is being met, and I encourage you to get curious about what that need is. Gaining such insights will empower you and may help you to understand what you are avoiding and why. Ultimately, at this stage you are deciding whether to break or sustain old patterns. In my view, this is the birthplace of meaningful change.

More importantly, what truly gets exposed here is your resistance to change. This is more gold. When you are fully WOKE and you know that you are selling yourself short, you are operating in fear. In fact, it is in this space that you come face to face with your fears - your fear of change, your fear of leaving your comfort zone, your fear of being alone, your fear of stepping out and standing up, your fear of the unknown, your fear of criticism, your fear of being a target, your fear of haters. These fears are often based on an imagined reality, a vivid fantasy that you conjure up in the crevices of your mind. Beyond the fear is possibility. Pushing through the fear is where you experience newness. Beyond the fear is where you discover more of who you truly are, and where you experience new and different aspects of yourself. Move beyond the fear and you may experience that you are worthy of so much more. Beyond the fear is where you experience more of your untapped potential. Experience the world. You really have no idea how great you are. Indulge that thought for a moment. It's immense: 'I am enough, I am worthy, I deserve better.' It's incredible. Soak it up. It's overwhelming. Let it wash all over you.

INTO THE FUTURE: EMBRACING CHANGE AND FINDING WORTHINESS

We are programmed to operate in fear. This is especially true if we have been an underdog or played small for most of our lives. When we try something new, the fear kicks in and we often retreat at breakneck speed back into the comforts of our logical head. We crave certainty and want a ten-step programme with detailed instructions about how to live our best life. Yet deep down, at gut level, we know that life doesn't work to a formula. Life has its own agenda. In the first instance, if we're serious about change and really want to 'level up', then we'll need to pay attention to where our energy goes. 'Where attention goes, energy flows.' So we must get focused and block out the noise. Our ability to manage distractions is key to our efforts to change. I am always fascinated when there is a stark discrepancy between behaviour and knowledge. Often self-sabotage is in the mix, and distraction is just one of many tools that Cruella de Vil will utilise to keep us 'playing small'. So monitor your behaviour on your smart phone. Because these devices can have us playing dumb.

When my clients arrive at a crossroads, when there is a conflict between words and deeds, my curiosity is aroused. I wholeheartedly believe in the process of change, even when we procrastinate and sell ourselves short. There is purpose hidden in that behaviour, if only we can uncover the true motives behind it. It's at this point that I wonder whether a person is ready to step up to the plate, really wants to take it to the next level. It's a good question to ask, a question that focuses the mind and goes straight to the heart of the block that hinders meaningful progress.

At times, when working therapeutically with deep-rooted self-sabotaging behaviours that evoke defenses and a resistance re-flux. It is easy to get distracted by that struggle and it can feel like hitting a brick wall. Over time, I have come to realise that unhelpful behaviour eventually burns itself out, if - and I hasten to add, if - the following process occurs. I call it 'planting seeds of newness'. When we make it our business to embrace new activities and interests, and take new uncharted directions, we start to make important self-love shifts. When we say yes to taking dance classes, yes to finally flying a kite, yes to taking a sign language course, yes to taking a four-month career break, yes to selling the house and moving somewhere new, yes to taking a new job in another town, city or country: in this sacred space of yes, where we invite newness, where we finally give ourselves permission, we begin to turn the tide. We push back. We build courage. We build confidence. We create new versions of ourselves. We become brave. We are self-loving warriors. In each new situation where we say yes, we get bolder, stronger, better. In doing so, we literally have less time and energy to invest in less fruitful pursuits. So, naturally, they fall by the wayside, where they just fizzle out of their own accord. No resistance. No fight. No great plan. No force. They simply die, as we no longer give them our attention - as our lives become filled with newness, and we experience more of the person that we are becoming.

So relax. Notice what you notice, feel what you feel, let go of resistance and see what naturally unfurls as you give yourself permission. You see, you have to show up first, you have to risk first, step outside your comfort zone first. This is where the true magic happens, just on the other side of your comfort zone. At this point, all your self-development pursuits start to fuse and as-similate, and an enigmatic power of its own comes over you. You begin to realise, to truly realise that you have power. You know it at a gut level. The power of your potential overwhelms you, but fret not: this power is what you have been seeking all your life. It has always been within you, waiting to be exposed to the light. Don't run. Don't retreat. Let the goodness sweep over you. Step wholeheartedly into your glory. You are a child of god, and playing small no longer serves you. You have finally arrived at the door where the majestic truth resides: worthiness.

Worthiness is what you truly seek. You are worthy. Believe it, with all your might. Indulge the notion, just for a moment. Worthiness. I hope your mind is blown. If you are worthy then you must surrender. Surrender to the greatness within you. Surrender the years of conditioning that stifled you. Surrender the 'I am not good-enough' ideology. Disentangle yourself. Rise up. Get a strong foothold. Declare: 'I am enough. I am worthy.' Worthiness, I am convinced, is at the heart of the matter. True worthiness. I want you to know that you are worthy: worthy of more, worthy of love, worthy of respect, worthy of honour. You are created by god, and god makes no mistakes. Know your worth. Honour your worth. Hold your head high and step out into your greatness. You are here for a reason. Find your purpose. Create a mission. Stand up and be counted. Make a way where there is no way. Be the change. Be a voice. Lead the way. Leave a legacy.

OUTRO

For all the people whom I have supported, whether in a professional helping role or as a human being experiencing planet earth, whether it's a prisoner on the Du Cane Road or a chief exec in a high-rise glass building, worthiness is at the heart of the matter.

We often don't know it. But unworthiness underpins much of what hurts and hinders us from stepping confidently into more of who we really are. We get caught up in scenarios and situations that undermine or belittle us. At some level, we know that we are worthy of more.

The root of it all is that we want to feel worthy. We want to feel that we are enough.

And we are enough! We are worthy!

If you fully come to believe and, crucially, to act in accordance with your new-found belief, if you are one of the lucky few that reaches this Nirvana and you fully reside in knowing your worth, then I salute you.

You are a magnificent representation of creation and potential personified, just as I am, as I come to know my own true worth. The greatest battle is within.

Know your worth.

Greatness is within.

You are more than enough!

NEXT STEPS

I hope that this book has inspired you to think, and has encouraged you to take action to enrich your life. If you have taken progressive steps, and a leap outside of your comfort zone, then please feel free to post pictures of your achievements to me at: keeley@key4change.com

Or visit my Key for Change Facebook page to share your stories. It would be a delight to hear from you and to witness the new frontiers that you encounter. That always gives me goose bumps.

If you want to know more about me or would like to have a a consultation, then please visit my website at keyforchange.com or keeleytaverner.com

I can also be found on Instagram: key4change.

It would be a privilege to journey with you.

Keeley Taverner is a British-Jamaican psychotherapist who started adulthood as a mother of two, working as a cashier at Ikea while feeling trapped in an abusive relationship with a narcissist. Raised by her single mother on a London council estate where 'schools housed us rather than engineer our minds for success', she left school with no qualifications, prospects, ambition or self-belief.

Self-help books were a solace, and one day, as she sorted through abandoned stock at the checkout, she experienced what she describes as a 'yellow bag' epiphany, when she heard her inner voice speaking to her loud and clear. 'Surely you can do better than this, Keeley?' She listened, hard, and step by step, brick by brick, she began rebuilding her life.

From women's refuge to fighting for a place at a university to coaching prisoners to running her own practice, Key for Change, Keeley has boldly, passionately and courageously defied the odds - and now she's on a mission to help others do the same.

Cover design by Daniel Watson

Printed in Great Britain
by Amazon